The Montessori

Lisa Nolan

Montessori for the Earth
PETALUMA, CA

Copyright © 2016 by Lisa Nolan.

All rights reserved. No part of this publication may be reproduced, distributed or transmitted in any form or by any means, including photocopying, recording, or other electronic or mechanical methods, without the prior written permission of the publisher, except in the case of brief quotations embodied in critical reviews and certain other noncommercial uses permitted by copyright law. For permission requests, write to the publisher, addressed "Attention: Permissions Coordinator," at the address below.

Montessori for the Earth
C/O Monkey Star Press
POB 5343
Petaluma, CA 94955
monkeystarpressbooks.com

Montessori Organizer by Lisa Nolan. -- 1st ed.

ISBN-10: 0983499519
ISBN-13: 978-0983499510

Book Layout ©2016 BookDesignTemplates.com

About This Organizer	*1*
Must-Haves for Twos and Threes	*3*
How to Give a Three-Period Lesson	*7*
Organize by Subjects	*11*
Practical Life	11
Sensorial	13
Language	15
Numbers/Counting	17
Geography	19
Botany/Plants	21
Zoology/Animals	23
Cultural Subjects	25
Science	27
Organize by Months of the Year	*29*
January	29
February	30
March	31
April	32
May	33
June	34
July	35
August	36
September	37
October	38
November	39
December	40
Organize by Seasons	*41*
Autumn, Fall	41
Winter	42
Spring	43
Summer	44
Organize by Themes	*45*
Materials	*47*

Inexpensive Materials I Would Like to Buy	47
Expensive Materials	48
DIY Easy Materials I Would Like to Make	49
PDFs, Printables to Download & Print	50
Recommended Montessori Sellers	52

Lessons I Have Given   53

YouTube Lessons to Watch   59

My Child's Interests   61

Milestones   67

Fine Motor: Writing	67
Gross/Large Motor	69
Reading	72
Math/Numbers/Counting	74

Home Environment   77

Family Room	77
Living Room	78
Child's Bedroom	79
Kitchen	80
Bathroom	81
Closet	82
School Room or Zone	83
Garage, Patio, or Deck	84
Backyard	85

Blogs of Interest   87

Books of Interest   89

Facebook Groups of Interest   91

Questions to Ask   93

About Lisa Nolan   95

About This Organizer

The *Montessori Organizer* is designed for moms who are beginning their journey into incorporating Montessori in their home environment! It is 90 pages long, black and white text, easy to use, go at your own pace, and created by a trained Montessori teacher and mom, Lisa Nolan of Montessori for the Earth and Confessions of a Montessori Mom. It includes a list of must-haves for two- and three-year olds, and a "how to" on giving a Three-Period Lesson.

The *Montessori Organizer* will organize by 1) Montessori subjects, 2) months of the year, 3) seasons, and 4) themes. You will be able to list 1) materials including DIY and printables, affordable, and expensive, 2) list Montessori sellers, 3) list lessons you have given, 3) list YouTube lessons to watch, 4) list rooms in the home environment, 5) list Montessori blogs, books, groups of interest, and much more!

This organizer is NOT a Montessori album. It does NOT include lessons or activities. It does NOT include images or photos. If you are interested in Montessori activities and lessons for birth to age nine, visit Montessori for the Earth.

I hope you enjoy our organizer! Feel free to contact me with any comments, feedback, and or suggestions!

~Lisa Nolan

Must-Haves for Twos and Threes

Practical Life

Sponges for cleaning spills:
- When to buy/make: your toddler has the fine motor skills to squeeze out a sponge.
- Test this skill at bath time or during outside water-table play.

Dry pouring activity:
- When to buy/make: your toddler shows an interest in pouring, especially while eating, like pouring out her cup of milk.
- Put out a dry pouring activity, then wait and see if your toddler shows any interest.
- Use large pasta or large objects for pouring, and test it out yourself, first.

Sensorial

Knobbed Cylinder Block(s):
- If you can't buy all four, buy the first one, sometimes called Cylinder Block A (the cylinders are the same height but differ in width from thick to thin).
- When to buy/make: your toddler places objects in baskets, drawers, containers, and or bags, and takes them out, repeatedly (including the laundry basket); he can do big-knobbed puzzles without a lot of frustration.

Pink Tower/Stacking Boxes:
- When to buy/make: your toddler stacks and or piles objects around the house, like books, blocks, containers, shoes, food containers, cups.
- If you don't want to afford a Pink Tower from a Montessori supplier, try an alternative stacking activity, like wooden stacking boxes (harder to use because they are hollow, so use three or four of the smaller ones to start out with).
- You can also buy decorated cardboard stacking boxes.

Art
Chalk and chalk board:
- When to buy/make: your toddler can pick up and hold a knobbed puzzle piece with ease; when markers, colored pencils, and crayons are still too hard for her to hold and manipulate.
- Note: markers are easier to put onto paper, followed by colored pencils. Crayons require a lot more fine motor strength.

Language
The Classified Picture Cards:
- When to buy/make: your toddler is hungry for the names of things around the house, points a lot to hear their names including pictures in books.
- Your toddler does not need to be speaking/speaking well.

Must-have Montessori Materials for Three-Year Olds and When to Buy/Make

Practical Life
Sponges for cleaning spills:
- When to buy/make: your three-year old has the fine motor skills to squeeze out a sponge.
- Test this skill at bath time or during outside water-table play.

Dry pouring activity:
- When to buy/make: your three-year old shows an interest in pouring, especially while eating, like pouring out her cup of juice.
- Put out a dry pouring activity, then wait and see if your three-year old shows any interest.
- Use large pasta or large objects for pouring, and test it out yourself, first.

Water pouring activity:
- When to buy/make: your three-year old shows an interest in pouring, especially while eating, like pouring out her cup of juice; your three-year old is potty training and or shows a growing affection for water (she spends a lot of time at the sink playing in the water during hand washing or sponge rinsing).
- Your three-year old is able to use a sponge (for wiping up spills).
- Put out a water pouring activity. Then wait and see if your three-year old shows any interest.
- Use food coloring for water pouring, and test it out yourself, first. You can change the color weekly or daily!

Spooning activity: you will need to try out different spoons to see what is best for your three-year old, including Chinese soup spoons, coffee scuppers, infant spoons, and so forth (so start collecting spoons). And if you child has difficulty with spooning, try spooning with water. (By the way, tongs are harder.)

Sensorial
Geometric Solids and Bases:
- When to buy: your child shows an interest in shape puzzles, shape sorters, and or the mystery Bag.
- Working with geometric shapes, bases, and later cards, is an indirect preparation for reading and writing as they train the child's eye to see and to distinguish lines (straight and circular) and geometric shapes, which correspond with the shapes of letters and numbers! So buy and or make as many activities as you can using geometric shapes including shape sorters, puzzles, sorting, drawing, tracing, stencils, exploring shapes in the home (a table is a rectangle, an ice cube is a cube, an ice cream scoop is a sphere) but make sure you use the correct terminology for shapes (both flat and 3D).

Geography
World Puzzle Map:
- When to buy: your child can do a small-knobbed puzzle with seven pieces (but by age four to learn the continent names, and animals from those continents).
- If you don't want to afford the Montessori World Puzzle Map (the one with all the continents) look for a floor puzzle that shows the world continents, or a jigsaw puzzle (both would be more advanced and more age appropriate for a four year old).

Language
I Spy:
- When to buy/make: age three.

Sandpaper Sounds/Letters:
- When to buy/make: after your child has played (had a lesson on) I Spy a few times.
- When your child wants to learn how to write her name.
- When your child shows an interest in drawing or writing.
- When your child is becoming more adept at art projects (painting, chalk board, using markers, collage, play dough).
- If they are already in the environment and your child asks for them; or takes them off the shelf to play/work with them.
- You just have a hunch.

Math

One of the following: *either* the Number Rods, Spindle Boxes, or the Color Bead Stair (*if* you do not want to afford all three).

Use one of the above, first, before you go on to introduce numbers (the Sandpaper Numbers).

Which should you choose?
- Number Rods: if your child loves the Pink Tower, stacking boxes, the Brown Stairs, and is good at sorting, is not able to count to ten, yet, and or enjoys working on a rug, go with the Number Rods (large or small).
- Spindle Boxes: if your child is already interested in numbers and can recognise a few, enjoys sorting objects, enjoys the Knobbed Cylinders, likes to sit in a chair and work at a table (although the Spindle Boxes can be done on a rug), can count to nine, and or can handle a lot of pieces at a time (some young children cannot handle too many pieces in an activity) . . . go with the Spindle Boxes.
- Color Bead Stair: if your child has strong fine motor skills, is precise, interested in small objects, works with beading materials, and can count from one to nine, go with the Colored Bead Stair.

Sandpaper Numbers:
- When to make/buy: when your child has worked a lot with either the Number Rods, Spindle Boxes, or the Color Bead Stair.
- When your child begins to recognize numbers.
- When your child shows an interest in drawing or writing.
- When your child is becoming more adept at art projects (painting, chalk board, using markers, collage, play dough).
- If they are already in the environment and your child asks for them; or takes them off the shelf to play/work with them.
- You just have a hunch.

How to Give a Three-Period Lesson

The Three-Period Lesson is a way to present and introduce concepts and "new terminology," or the names of things, to a child: new sounds (letters), numbers (symbols), geometric shapes, colors, and geography forms (like the Land and Water Forms or the continents). It is also a way to enrich the child's vocabulary. The technique was originated by Edouard Sequin, a French educator from the 1800s.

There are three stages to the Three-Period Lesson: the first stage, also called the First Period, is the Association or Recognition of Identity Stage. It is an introduction of names and or concepts to the child. In the example lesson below, the names of three color tablets (from the Color Tablets, box one) are introduced to the child: blue, red, and yellow. The names of the objects are introduced by the adult into the consciousness of the child: "This is red. This is blue. And this is yellow." In this First Period, the child is making an association with the object and the name of that object.

In the Second Period, called the Recognition of Contrasts Stage, the names are repeated to the child who can now interact with the objects (in our example, the Color Tablets). In this Second Period, the child has an opportunity to demonstrate his new knowledge of the names or concepts that were just introduced to him by showing you (or holding up) the object when asked for it. The child is still given the names of the objects, but he has to show you which is the correct one by picking it up and handing it to you: "Can you give me the red tablet? Can you give me the yellow tablet? Can you give me the blue tablet?"

The Third Period is the Consolidation Stage, the child is asked to name the Color Tablets all on his own, to pull from his mind and into consciousness, the names of the objects (or the colors of the color tablets as in our example). In this period, the child will show the adult whether or not he can identify the names of the new objects, concepts, letters, or numbers, as well as pronounce them correctly.

Few words are spoken during the Three-Period Lesson, so as to better isolate the terms or names (blue, red, and yellow for example) that are being introduced and taught to the child.

It is important that the three objects chosen for a Three-Period Lesson be contrasting, or different from each other. For example, presenting the letters "b" and "d" for the first time to a child would not be wise as they are so similar in shape; or the numbers six and nine.

The Three-Period Lesson can also be used by the adult to test the child's knowledge of the names of things (like colors, numbers, letters, animals, etc.) by asking the child, "What is this?" This is used a lot when teaching a child the letters of the alphabet or numbers. If, for example, you gave a Three-Period Lesson on the numbers "one," "two," and "three" on Monday, you would test the child on Tuesday to see if he remembered the names of the numbers. If he did not remember any of them, you would repeat the Three-Period Lesson. If he remembered the "one," for example, but not the "two" or "three," you could either repeat the lesson on just the "two" and the "three," or introduce the number "four" and give a Three-Period Lesson on the "two," "three," and "four." If the child remembered the "one" and the "two," but not the "three," you could either give a lesson on the "two" and "three" or introduce the "four" and the "five" and give a lesson on the "three," "four," and the "five." It is sometimes best to give one familiar object along with two new objects in your Three-Period Lesson.

Three-period lessons given to toddlers and young threes, or children, are sometimes done with only two objects. Both objects can be new (unknown to the child) or one can be familiar and one can be new.

Materials: Small Number Rods (after the child knows how to put them in order from one to ten or one to five).

First Period:
1. Take the one, two, and three rods. Isolate them on the mat. Place one rod in front of the child. "This is one." (Touch your fingers on the red one rod as you say one.) "Would you like to count?" Child: "One."
2. Place the second rod in front of the child. "This is two: One, two." (Touch your fingers on the red as you say one and the blue as you say two, and count from left to right.) "Would you like to count?" Child: "One, two."
3. Place the third rod in front of the child. "This is three. One, two, three," (touching all three sections, one color at time). "Would you like to count?" Child: "One, two, three."
*Help the child to count the Number Rods with their open hand with palms down, touching each section, one color at time, from left to right, from red to blue.

Second Period:
1. Ask the child, "Give me the two please," child counts the Number Rods looking for the two rod, and hands you the two rod. "Thank you." Say to the child, "Let's count it. One, two." (Remember to touch the colors as you count.)
2. "Give me the one please," child counts the Number Rods looking for the one rod, and hands you the one rod. "Thank you. Let's count it. One." (Remember to touch the colors as you count.)
3. "Give me three please," child counts the Number Rods looking for the three rod, and hands you the three rod. "Thank you. Let's count it. One, two, three." (Remember to touch the colors as you count.)

Third Period:
1. Hold up the two rod ask child "What is this?" Child says: "Two."
2. Hold up the one rod ask child "What is this?" Child says: "One."
3. Hold up the three rod ask child "What is this?" Child says: "Three."

You can go on to the next three rods (number four, five, and six) if the child is interested, or wait until the next day--but review the rods you introduced the day before.

Question: Should you refrain from talking during a lesson? *I have read that during a Montessori presentation the teacher should not speak so as to not distract the child, and when the child is working the adult should not interrupt him. My question is: when and how is the language introduced? For example for cylinder blocks: thick and thin.* After having a child with Down syndrome, who has severe language delays, I am not so strict about this issue of not talking to the child during a presentation. My son needed a lot of language repeated over and over.

I think there is a separate issue about interrupting a child when they are working on a material independently (and you are not giving them a lesson).

But when you are giving a lesson, language can always be included. If you are doing the Knobbed Cylinder Block, for example, just point to the cylinder, touch it lightly and say "thick" then ask the child to touch it and repeat "thick." Do the same for "thin."

And let those concepts guide you through the day by pointing out thick and thin food or objects (thick banana, thin cracker for example).

Organize by Subjects

Practical Life

Activities to Make

Name (of activity):
Age (appropriate age group):
Materials needed:
Comments:

Name:
Age:
Materials needed:
Comments:

Name:
Age:
Materials needed:
Comments:

Name:
Age:
Materials needed:
Comments:

Name:
Age:
Materials needed:
Comments:

Activities to Buy

Name (of activity):
Age (appropriate age group):
Cost:
Comments:

Name:
Age:
Cost:
Comments:

Name:
Age:
Cost:
Comments:

Name:
Age:
Cost:
Comments:

Name:
Age:
Cost:
Comments:

Name:
Age:
Cost:
Comments:

Sensorial

Activities to Make

Name (of activity):
Age (appropriate age group):
Materials:
Comments:

Name:
Age:
Materials needed:
Comments:

Name:
Age:
Materials needed:
Comments:

Name:
Age:
Materials needed:
Comments:

Name:
Age:
Materials needed:
Comments:

Name:
Age:
Materials needed:
Comments:

Activities to Buy

Name (of activity):
Age (appropriate age group):
Cost:
Comments:

Name:
Age:
Cost:
Comments:

Name:
Age:
Cost:
Comments:

Name:
Age:
Cost:
Comments:

Name:
Age:
Cost:
Comments:

Name:
Age:
Cost:
Comments:

Language

Activities to Make

Name (of activity):
Age (appropriate age group):
Materials needed:
Comments:

Name:
Age:
Materials needed:
Comments:

Name:
Age:
Materials needed:
Comments:

Name:
Age:
Materials needed:
Comments:

Name:
Age:
Materials needed:
Comments:

Name:
Age:
Materials needed:
Comments:

Activities to Buy

Name (of activity):
Age (appropriate age group):
Cost:
Comments:

Name:
Age:
Cost:
Comments:

Name:
Age:
Cost:
Comments:

Name:
Age:
Cost:
Comments:

Name:
Age:
Cost:
Comments:

Name:
Age:
Cost:
Comments:

Numbers/Counting

Activities to Make

Name (of activity):
Age (appropriate age group):
Materials needed:
Comments:

Name:
Age:
Materials needed:
Comments:

Name:
Age:
Materials needed:
Comments:

Name:
Age:
Materials needed:
Comments:

Name:
Age:
Materials needed:
Comments:

Name:
Age:
Materials needed:
Comments:

Activities to Buy Name:
Age:
Cost:
Comments:

Name:
Age:
Cost:
Comments:

Name:
Age:
Cost:
Comments:

Name:
Age:
Cost:
Comments:

Name:
Age:
Cost:
Comments:

Name:
Age:
Cost:
Comments:

Geography

Activities to Make

Name (of activity):
Age (appropriate age group):
Materials needed:
Comments:

Name:
Age:
Materials needed:
Comments:

Name:
Age:
Materials needed:
Comments:

Name:
Age:
Materials needed:
Comments:

Name:
Age:
Materials needed:
Comments:

Name:
Age:
Materials needed:
Comments:

Activities to Buy

Name (of activity):
Age (appropriate age group):
Cost:
Comments:

Name:
Age:
Cost:
Comments:

Name:
Age:
Cost:
Comments:

Name:
Age:
Cost:
Comments:

Name:
Age:
Cost:
Comments:

Name:
Age:
Cost:
Comments:

Botany/Plants

Activities to Make

Name (of activity):
Age (appropriate age group):
Materials needed:
Comments:

Name:
Age:
Materials needed:
Comments:

Name:
Age:
Materials needed:
Comments:

Name:
Age:
Materials needed:
Comments:

Name:
Age:
Materials needed:
Comments:

Name:
Age:
Materials needed:
Comments:

Activities to Buy

Name (of activity):
Age (appropriate age group):
Cost:
Comments:

Name:
Age:
Cost:
Comments:

Name:
Age:
Cost:
Comments:

Name:
Age:
Cost:
Comments:

Name:
Age:
Cost:
Comments:

Name:
Age:
Cost:
Comments:

Zoology/Animals

Activities to Make

Name (of activity):
Age (appropriate age group):
Materials needed:
Comments:

Name:
Age:
Materials needed:
Comments:

Name:
Age:
Materials needed:
Comments:

Name:
Age:
Materials needed:
Comments:

Name:
Age:
Materials needed:
Comments:

Name:
Age:
Materials needed:
Comments:

Activities to Buy

Name (of activity):
Age (appropriate age group):
Cost:
Comments:

Name:
Age:
Cost:
Comments:

Name:
Age:
Cost:
Comments:

Name:
Age:
Cost:
Comments:

Name:
Age:
Cost:
Comments:

Name:
Age:
Cost:
Comments:

Cultural Subjects

Activities to Make

Name (of activity):
Age (appropriate age group):
Materials needed:
Comments:

Name:
Age:
Materials needed:
Comments:

Name:
Age:
Materials needed:
Comments:

Name:
Age:
Materials needed:
Comments:

Name:
Age:
Materials needed:
Comments:

Name:
Age:
Materials needed:
Comments:

Activities to Buy

Name (of activity):
Age (appropriate age group):
Cost:
Comments:

Name:
Age:
Cost:
Comments:

Name:
Age:
Cost:
Comments:

Name:
Age:
Cost:
Comments:

Name:
Age:
Cost:
Comments:

Name:
Age:
Cost:
Comments:

Science

Activities to Make:

Name (of activity):
Age (appropriate age group):
Materials needed:
Comments:

Name:
Age:
Materials needed:
Comments:

Name:
Age:
Materials needed:
Comments:

Name:
Age:
Materials needed:
Comments:

Name:
Age:
Materials needed:
Comments:

Name:
Age:
Materials needed:
Comments:

Activities to Buy

Name (of activity):
Age (appropriate age group):
Cost:
Comments:

Name:
Age:
Cost:
Comments:

Name:
Age:
Cost:
Comments:

Name:
Age:
Cost:
Comments:

Name:
Age:
Cost:
Comments:

Name:
Age:
Cost:
Comments:

Organize by Months of the Year

January

Subjects to Study

- ❖ Name of subject:
- ❖ Name of subject:
- ❖ Name of subject:
- ❖ Name of subject:
- ❖ Name of subject:
- ❖ Name of subject:

Themes

- ❖ Name of theme:
- ❖ Name of theme:
- ❖ Name of theme:
- ❖ Name of theme:
- ❖ Name of theme:
- ❖ Name of theme:
- ❖ Name of theme:

February

Subjects to Study

- ❖ Name of subject:

- ❖ Name of subject:

- ❖ Name of subject:

- ❖ Name of subject:

- ❖ Name of subject:

- ❖ Name of subject:

Themes

- ❖ Name of theme:

- ❖ Name of theme:

- ❖ Name of theme:

- ❖ Name of theme:

- ❖ Name of theme:

- ❖ Name of theme:

- ❖ Name of theme:

March

Subjects to Study

- ❖ Name of subject:

- ❖ Name of subject:

- ❖ Name of subject:

- ❖ Name of subject:

- ❖ Name of subject:

- ❖ Name of subject:

Themes

- ❖ Name of theme:

- ❖ Name of theme:

- ❖ Name of theme:

- ❖ Name of theme:

- ❖ Name of theme:

- ❖ Name of theme:

- ❖ Name of theme:

April

Subjects to Study

- ❖ Name of subject:

- ❖ Name of subject:

- ❖ Name of subject:

- ❖ Name of subject:

- ❖ Name of subject:

- ❖ Name of subject:

Themes

- ❖ Name of theme:

- ❖ Name of theme:

- ❖ Name of theme:

- ❖ Name of theme:

- ❖ Name of theme:

- ❖ Name of theme:

- ❖ Name of theme:

May

Subjects to Study

- ❖ Name of subject:

- ❖ Name of subject:

- ❖ Name of subject:

- ❖ Name of subject:

- ❖ Name of subject:

- ❖ Name of subject:

Themes

- ❖ Name of theme:

- ❖ Name of theme:

- ❖ Name of theme:

- ❖ Name of theme:

- ❖ Name of theme:

- ❖ Name of theme:

June

Subjects to Study

- ❖ Name of subject:

- ❖ Name of subject:

- ❖ Name of subject:

- ❖ Name of subject:

- ❖ Name of subject:

- ❖ Name of subject:

Themes

- ❖ Name of theme:

- ❖ Name of theme:

- ❖ Name of theme:

- ❖ Name of theme:

- ❖ Name of theme:

- ❖ Name of theme:

- ❖ Name of theme:

July

Subjects to Study

- ❖ Name of subject:

- ❖ Name of subject:

- ❖ Name of subject:

- ❖ Name of subject:

- ❖ Name of subject:

- ❖ Name of subject:

Themes

- ❖ Name of theme:

- ❖ Name of theme:

- ❖ Name of theme:

- ❖ Name of theme:

- ❖ Name of theme:

- ❖ Name of theme:

- ❖ Name of theme:

August

Subjects to Study

- ❖ Name of subject:

- ❖ Name of subject:

- ❖ Name of subject:

- ❖ Name of subject:

- ❖ Name of subject:

- ❖ Name of subject:

Themes

- ❖ Name of theme:

- ❖ Name of theme:

- ❖ Name of theme:

- ❖ Name of theme:

- ❖ Name of theme:

- ❖ Name of theme:

- ❖ Name of theme:

September

Subjects to Study

- ❖ Name of subject:

- ❖ Name of subject:

- ❖ Name of subject:

- ❖ Name of subject:

- ❖ Name of subject:

- ❖ Name of subject:

Themes

- ❖ Name of theme:

- ❖ Name of theme:

- ❖ Name of theme:

- ❖ Name of theme:

- ❖ Name of theme:

- ❖ Name of theme:

October

Subjects to Study

- ❖ Name of subject:
- ❖ Name of subject:
- ❖ Name of subject:
- ❖ Name of subject:
- ❖ Name of subject:
- ❖ Name of subject:

Themes

- ❖ Name of theme:
- ❖ Name of theme:
- ❖ Name of theme:
- ❖ Name of theme:
- ❖ Name of theme:
- ❖ Name of theme:
- ❖ Name of theme:

November

Subjects to Study

- ❖ Name of subject:

- ❖ Name of subject:

- ❖ Name of subject:

- ❖ Name of subject:

- ❖ Name of subject:

- ❖ Name of subject:

Themes

- ❖ Name of theme:

- ❖ Name of theme:

- ❖ Name of theme:

- ❖ Name of theme:

- ❖ Name of theme:

- ❖ Name of theme:

- ❖ Name of theme:

December

Subjects to Study

- ❖ Name of subject:

- ❖ Name of subject:

- ❖ Name of subject:

- ❖ Name of subject:

- ❖ Name of subject:

- ❖ Name of subject:

Themes

- ❖ Name of theme:

- ❖ Name of theme:

- ❖ Name of theme:

- ❖ Name of theme:

- ❖ Name of theme:

- ❖ Name of theme:

- ❖ Name of theme:

Organize by Seasons

Autumn, Fall

Subjects to Study

- ❖ Name of subject:

- ❖ Name of subject:

- ❖ Name of subject:

- ❖ Name of subject:

- ❖ Name of subject:

- ❖ Name of subject:

Themes

- ❖ Name of theme:

- ❖ Name of theme:

- ❖ Name of theme:

- ❖ Name of theme:

- ❖ Name of theme:

- ❖ Name of theme:

- ❖ Name of theme:

Winter

Subjects to Study

- ❖ Name of subject:

- ❖ Name of subject:

- ❖ Name of subject:

- ❖ Name of subject:

- ❖ Name of subject:

- ❖ Name of subject:

Themes

- ❖ Name of theme:

- ❖ Name of theme:

- ❖ Name of theme:

- ❖ Name of theme:

- ❖ Name of theme:

- ❖ Name of theme:

- ❖ Name of theme:

Spring

Subjects to Study

- ❖ Name of subject:

- ❖ Name of subject:

- ❖ Name of subject:

- ❖ Name of subject:

- ❖ Name of subject:

- ❖ Name of subject:

Themes

- ❖ Name of theme:

- ❖ Name of theme:

- ❖ Name of theme:

- ❖ Name of theme:

- ❖ Name of theme:

- ❖ Name of theme:

- ❖ Name of theme:

Summer

Subjects to Study

- ❖ Name of subject:

- ❖ Name of subject:

- ❖ Name of subject:

- ❖ Name of subject:

- ❖ Name of subject:

- ❖ Name of subject:

Themes

- ❖ Name of theme:

- ❖ Name of theme:

- ❖ Name of theme:

- ❖ Name of theme:

- ❖ Name of theme:

- ❖ Name of theme:

- ❖ Name of theme:

Organize by Themes

Name of theme:
Age/s:
Comments:

Name of theme:
Age/s:
Comments:

Name of theme:
Age/s:
Comments:

Name of theme:
Age/s:
Comments:

Name of theme:
Age/s:
Comments:

Name of theme:
Age/s:
Comments:

Name of theme:
Age/s:
Comments:

Name of theme:
Age/s:
Comments:

Name of theme:
Age/s:
Comments:

Name of theme:
Age/s:
Comments:

Name of theme:
Age/s:
Comments:

Name of theme:
Age/s:
Comments:

Materials

Inexpensive Materials I Would Like to Buy

Name of material/activity:
Where to buy:
Cost:
Shipping:
Comments:

Name of material/activity:
Where to buy:
Cost:
Shipping:
Comments:

Name of material/activity:
Where to buy:
Cost:
Shipping:
Comments:

Name of material/activity:
Where to buy:
Cost:
Shipping:
Comments:

Name of material/activity:
Where to buy:
Cost:
Shipping:
Comments:

Expensive Materials

Name of material/activity:
Where to buy:
Cost:
Shipping:
Comments:

Name of material/activity:
Where to buy:
Cost:
Shipping:
Comments:

Name of material/activity:
Where to buy:
Cost:
Shipping:
Comments:

Name of material/activity:
Where to buy:
Cost:
Shipping:
Comments:

Name of material/activity:
Where to buy:
Cost:
Shipping:
Comments:

Name of material/activity:
Where to buy:
Cost:
Shipping:
Comments:

DIY Easy Materials I Would Like to Make

Name of material/activity:
Materials needed:

Comments:

Name of material/activity:
Materials needed:

Comments:

Name of material/activity:
Materials needed:

Comments:

Name of material/activity:
Materials needed:

Comments:

Name of material/activity:
Materials needed:

Comments:

Name of material/activity:
Materials needed:

Comments:

PDFs, Printables to Download & Print

Name of PDF/printable and cost:
Name of seller or blog:
Link/URL:
Comments:

Name of PDF/printable and cost:
Name of seller or blog:
Link/URL:
Comments:

Name of PDF/printable and cost:
Name of seller or blog:
Link/URL:
Comments:

Name of PDF/printable and cost:
Name of seller or blog:
Link/URL:
Comments:

Name of PDF/printable and cost:
Name of seller or blog:
Link/URL:
Comments:

Name of PDF/printable and cost:
Name of seller or blog:
Link/URL:
Comments:

Name of PDF/printable and cost:
Name of seller or blog:
Link/URL:
Comments:

Name of PDF/printable and cost:
Name of seller or blog:
Link/URL:
Comments:

Name of PDF/printable and cost:
Name of seller or blog:
Link/URL:
Comments:

Name of PDF/printable and cost:
Name of seller or blog:
Link/URL:
Comments:

Name of PDF/printable and cost:
Name of seller or blog:
Link/URL:
Comments:

Name of PDF/printable and cost:
Name of seller or blog:
Link/URL:
Comments:

Name of PDF/printable and cost:
Name of seller or blog:
Link/URL:
Comments:

Name of PDF/printable and cost:
Name of seller or blog:
Link/URL:
Comments:

Recommended Montessori Sellers

Name of seller or blog:
Address or link/URL:
Shipping Costs:
Comments:

Name of seller or blog:
Address or link/URL:
Shipping Costs:
Comments:

Name of seller or blog:
Address or link/URL:
Shipping Costs:
Comments:

Name of seller or blog:
Address or link/URL:
Shipping Costs:
Comments:

Name of seller or blog:
Address or link/URL:
Shipping Costs:
Comments:

Name of seller or blog:
Address or link/URL:
Shipping Costs:
Comments:

Name of seller or blog:
Address or link/URL:
Shipping Costs:
Comments:

Lessons I Have Given

Child's Name

Lesson and subject:
Date:
Need to re present___ mastered___.
Comments:

Lesson and subject:
Date:
Need to re present___ mastered___.
Comments:

Lesson and subject:
Date:
Need to re present___ mastered___.
Comments:

Lesson and subject:
Date:
Need to re present___ mastered___.
Comments:

Lesson and subject:
Date:
Need to re present___ mastered___.
Comments:

Lesson and subject:
Date:
Need to re present___ mastered___.
Comments:

Lesson and subject:
Date:
Need to re present___ mastered___.
Comments:

Lesson and subject:
Date:
Need to re present___ mastered___.
Comments:

Lesson and subject:
Date:
Need to re present___ mastered___.
Comments:

Lesson and subject:
Date:
Need to re present___ mastered___.
Comments:

Lesson and subject:
Date:
Need to re present___ mastered___.
Comments:

Child's Name

Lesson and subject:
Date:
Need to re present___ mastered___.
Comments:

Lesson and subject:
Date:
Need to re present___ mastered___.
Comments:

Lesson and subject:
Date:
Need to re present___ mastered___.
Comments:

Lesson and subject:
Date:
Need to re present___ mastered___.
Comments:

Lesson and subject:
Date:
Need to re present___ mastered___.
Comments:

Lesson and subject:
Date:
Need to re present___ mastered___.
Comments:

Lesson and subject:
Date:
Need to re present___ mastered___.
Comments:

Lesson and subject:
Date:
Need to re present___ mastered___.
Comments:

Lesson and subject:
Date:
Need to re present___ mastered___.
Comments:

Lesson and subject:
Date:
Need to re present___ mastered___.
Comments:

Lesson and subject:
Date:
Need to re present___ mastered___.
Comments:

Lesson and subject:
Date:
Need to re present___ mastered___.
Comments:

Child's Name

Lesson and subject:
Date:
Need to re present___ mastered___.
Comments:

Lesson and subject:
Date:
Need to re present___ mastered___.
Comments:

Lesson and subject:
Date:
Need to re present___ mastered___.
Comments:

Lesson and subject:
Date:
Need to re present___ mastered___.
Comments:

Lesson and subject:
Date:
Need to re present___ mastered___.
Comments:

Lesson and subject:
Date:
Need to re present___ mastered___.
Comments:

Lesson and subject:
Date:
Need to re present___ mastered___.
Comments:

Lesson and subject:
Date:
Need to re present___ mastered___.
Comments:

Lesson and subject:
Date:
Need to re present___ mastered___.
Comments:

Lesson and subject:
Date:
Need to re present___ mastered___.
Comments:

Lesson and subject:
Date:
Need to re present___ mastered___.
Comments:

Lesson and subject:
Date:
Need to re present___ mastered___.
Comments:

YouTube Lessons to Watch

Name of presenter, their blog or website:
Name of video:
Subject, lesson:
Age/s:
Channel (to subscribe to):
Comments:

Name of presenter, their blog or website:
Name of video:
Subject, lesson:
Age/s:
Channel (to subscribe to):
Comments:

Name of presenter, their blog or website:
Name of video:
Subject, lesson:
Age/s:
Channel (to subscribe to):
Comments:

Name of presenter, their blog or website:
Name of video:
Subject, lesson:
Age/s:
Channel (to subscribe to):
Comments:

Name of presenter, their blog or website:
Name of video:
Subject, lesson:
Age/s:
Channel (to subscribe to):
Comments:

Name of presenter, their blog or website:
Name of video:
Subject, lesson:
Age/s:
Channel (to subscribe to):
Comments:

Name of presenter, their blog or website:
Name of video:
Subject, lesson:
Age/s:
Channel (to subscribe to):
Comments:

Name of presenter, their blog or website:
Name of video:
Subject, lesson:
Age/s:
Channel (to subscribe to):
Comments:

Name of presenter, their blog or website:
Name of video:
Subject, lesson:
Age/s:
Channel (to subscribe to):
Comments:

My Child's Interests

Name of Child

Age:
Date:
Name of subject, material, lesson, or theme of interest:
Comments:

Age:
Date:
Name of subject, material, lesson, or theme of interest:
Comments:

Age:
Date:
Name of subject, material, lesson, or theme of interest:
Comments:

Age:
Date:
Name of subject, material, lesson, or theme of interest:
Comments:

Age:
Date:
Name of subject, material, lesson, or theme of interest:
Comments:

Age:
Date:
Name of subject, material, lesson, or theme of interest:
Comments:

Age:
Date:
Name of subject, material, lesson, or theme of interest:
Comments:

Age:
Date:
Name of subject, material, lesson, or theme of interest:
Comments:

Age:
Date:
Name of subject, material, lesson, or theme of interest:
Comments:

Age:
Date:
Name of subject, material, lesson, or theme of interest:
Comments:

Age:
Date:
Name of subject, material, lesson, or theme of interest:
Comments:

Name of Child

Age:
Date:
Name of subject, material, lesson, or theme of interest:
Comments:

Age:
Date:
Name of subject, material, lesson, or theme of interest:
Comments:

Age:
Date:
Name of subject, material, lesson, or theme of interest:
Comments:

Age:
Date:
Name of subject, material, lesson, or theme of interest:
Comments:

Age:
Date:
Name of subject, material, lesson, or theme of interest:
Comments:

Age:
Date:
Name of subject, material, lesson, or theme of interest:
Comments:

Age:
Date:
Name of subject, material, lesson, or theme of interest:
Comments:

Age:
Date:
Name of subject, material, lesson, or theme of interest:
Comments:

Age:
Date:
Name of subject, material, lesson, or theme of interest:
Comments:

Age:
Date:
Name of subject, material, lesson, or theme of interest:
Comments:

Age:
Date:
Name of subject, material, lesson, or theme of interest:
Comments:

Age:
Date:
Name of subject, material, lesson, or theme of interest:
Comments:

Name of Child

Age:
Date:
Name of subject, material, lesson, or theme of interest:
Comments:

Age:
Date:
Name of subject, material, lesson, or theme of interest:
Comments:

Age:
Date:
Name of subject, material, lesson, or theme of interest:
Comments:

Age:
Date:
Name of subject, material, lesson, or theme of interest:
Comments:

Age:
Date:
Name of subject, material, lesson, or theme of interest:
Comments:

Age:
Date:
Name of subject, material, lesson, or theme of interest:
Comments:

Age:
Date:
Name of subject, material, lesson, or theme of interest:
Comments:

Age:
Date:
Name of subject, material, lesson, or theme of interest:
Comments:

Age:
Date:
Name of subject, material, lesson, or theme of interest:
Comments:

Age:
Date:
Name of subject, material, lesson, or theme of interest:
Comments:

Age:
Date:
Name of subject, material, lesson, or theme of interest:
Comments:

Age:
Date:
Name of subject, material, lesson, or theme of interest:
Comments:

Milestones

Fine Motor: Writing

Writes Numbers

Name and age of child:
Date:
Comments:

Name and age of child:
Date:
Comments:

Name and age of child:
Date:
Comments:

Writes Name

Name and age of child:
Date:
Comments:

Name and age of child:
Date:
Comments:

Name and age of child:
Date:
Comments:

Writes Letters of the Alphabet

Name and age of child:
Date:
Comments:

Name and age of child:
Date:
Comments:

Name and age of child:
Date:
Comments:

Gross/Large Motor

Walks Heel to Toe on a Line

Name and age of child:
Date:
Comments:

Name and age of child:
Date:
Comments:

Name and age of child:
Date:
Comments:

Jumps

Name and age of child:
Date:
Comments:

Name and age of child:
Date:
Comments:

Name and age of child:
Date:
Comments:

Hops

Name and age of child:
Date:
Comments:

Name and age of child:
Date:
Comments:

Name and age of child:
Date:
Comments:

Runs

Name and age of child:
Date:
Comments:

Name and age of child:
Date:
Comments:

Name and age of child:
Date:
Comments:

Skips

Name and age of child:
Date:
Comments:

Name and age of child:
Date:
Comments:

Name and age of child:
Date:
Comments:

Reading

Reads Phonetically

Name and age of child:
Date:
Comments:

Name and age of child:
Date:
Comments:

Name and age of child:
Date:
Comments:

Reads Sight Words

Name and age of child:
Date:
Comments:

Name and age of child:
Date:
Comments:

Name and age of child:
Date:
Comments:

Reads Whole Language

Name and age of child:
Date:
Comments:

Name and age of child:
Date:
Comments:

Name and age of child:
Date:
Comments:

Math/Numbers/Counting

Counts to 10 & Number Rods

Name and age of child:
Date:
Comments:

Name and age of child:
Date:
Comments:

Name and age of child:
Date:
Comments:

SP Numbers & Recognizes 1 to 10

Name and age of child:
Date:
Comments:

Name and age of child:
Date:
Comments:

Name and age of child:
Date:
Comments:

Counts to 20 & Teen Beads

Name and age of child:
Date:
Comments:

Name and age of child:
Date:
Comments:

Name and age of child:
Date:
Comments:

Color Bead Stair

Name and age of child:
Date:
Comments:

Name and age of child:
Date:
Comments:

Name and age of child:
Date:
Comments:

Home Environment

Family Room

What to buy:

What to make:

What to save up for:

Living Room

What to buy:

What to make:

What to save up for:

Child's Bedroom

What to buy:

What to make:

What to save up for:

Kitchen

What to buy:

What to make:

What to save up for:

Bathroom

What to buy:

What to make:

What to save up for:

Closet

What to buy:

What to make:

What to save up for:

School Room or Zone

What to buy:

What to make:

What to save up for:

Garage, Patio, or Deck

What to buy:

What to make:

What to save up for:

Backyard

What to buy:

What to make:

What to save up for:

Blogs of Interest

Name of blog:
Name of blogger:
URL, link to blog:
Comments:

Name of blog:
Name of blogger:
URL, link to blog:
Comments:

Name of blog:
Name of blogger:
URL, link to blog:
Comments:

Name of blog:
Name of blogger:
URL, link to blog:
Comments:

Name of blog:
Name of blogger:
URL, link to blog:
Comments:

Name of blog:
Name of blogger:
URL, link to blog:
Comments:

Name of blog:
Name of blogger:
URL, link to blog:
Comments:

Name of blog:
Name of blogger:
URL, link to blog:
Comments:

Name of blog:
Name of blogger:
URL, link to blog:
Comments:

Name of blog:
Name of blogger:
URL, link to blog:
Comments:

Name of blog:
Name of blogger:
URL, link to blog:
Comments:

Books of Interest

Name of book:
Name of author:
URL, link to book:
Comments:

Name of book:
Name of author:
URL, link to book:
Comments:

Name of book:
Name of author:
URL, link to book:
Comments:

Name of book:
Name of author:
URL, link to book:
Comments:

Name of book:
Name of author:
URL, link to book:
Comments:

Name of book:
Name of author:
URL, link to book:
Comments:

Name of book:
Name of author:
URL, link to book:
Comments:

Name of book:
Name of author:
URL, link to book:
Comments:

Name of book:
Name of author:
URL, link to book:
Comments:

Name of book:
Name of author:
URL, link to book:
Comments:

Name of book:
Name of author:
URL, link to book:
Comments:

Facebook Groups of Interest

Name of group:
Name of admin/host:
URL, link to group:
Comments:

Name of group:
Name of admin/host:
URL, link to group:
Comments:

Name of group:
Name of admin/host:
URL, link to group:
Comments:

Name of group:
Name of admin/host:
URL, link to group:
Comments:

Name of group:
Name of admin/host:
URL, link to group:
Comments:

Name of group:
Name of admin/host:
URL, link to group:
Comments:

Name of group:
Name of admin/host:
URL, link to group:
Comments:

Name of group:
Name of admin/host:
URL, link to group:
Comments:

Name of group:
Name of admin/host:
URL, link to group:
Comments:

Name of group:
Name of admin/host:
URL, link to group:
Comments:

Name of group:
Name of admin/host:
URL, link to group:
Comments:

Questions to Ask

The subject:
Name of the lesson, material, or activity:
Age of your child:
Your question:

Answers/Feedback:

The subject:
Name of the lesson, material, or activity:
Age of your child:
Your question:

Answers/Feedback:

The subject:
Name of the lesson, material, or activity:
Age of your child:
Your question:

Answers/Feedback:

The subject:
Name of the lesson, material, or activity:
Age of your child:
Your question:

Answers/Feedback:

The subject:
Name of the lesson, material, or activity:
Age of your child:
Your question:

Answers/Feedback:

The subject:
Name of the lesson, material, or activity:
Age of your child:
Your question:

Answers/Feedback:

The subject:
Name of the lesson, material, or activity:
Age of your child:
Your question:

Answers/Feedback:

The subject:
Name of the lesson, material, or activity:
Age of your child:
Your question:

Answers/Feedback:

About Lisa Nolan

Lisa Nolan is a trained and certified 3 to 6 and 6 to 9 Montessori teacher. She has taught Montessori in the San Francisco Bay Area since 1986. She took her Montessori primary training in 1986 at The Maria Montessori School of the Golden Gate in San Francisco with the late headmistress, Ursula Thrush. She then took her Montessori lower elementary training 1988 at The Maria Montessori School of the Golden Gate in San Francisco through the University Extension, University of California Berkeley. Ms. Nolan is also an editor, a publisher, a stay-at-home and work-at-home mom, a webmaster, and a blogger. She received an MA from San Francisco State University. After her son was born with Down syndrome in 2004, Lisa Nolan has used Montessori concepts and principles for his education since his birth. She has been involved and committed to the field of early childhood education since 1982 when, as a college student, she interned at a local Head Start preschool. This experience gave her more joy than any job she ever had (at the ripe age of 20). A few years later, remembering that experience, she began working as a teacher's assistant at a local preschool. One year later she was hired as an assistant in the toddler classroom at a Montessori school. She took her Montessori primary training at the same time (and later her lower elementary Montessori training). In 1993, while in graduate school, she founded and directed a children's theater program at the Marsh, a local theater in San Francisco, developing matinees and classes for young children. In 1998 she took her teaching experience and Montessori training to the Internet and created her website, Montessori for the Earth, offering affordable Montessori online programs to parents, teachers, and homeschoolers. During the years that followed, she left the field of early childhood education several times, only to return again because no other field gives her such joy and satisfaction.

Lisa Nolan blogs at Confessions of a Montessori Mom and Montessori on a Budget. You can reach Lisa Nolan through her website: LisaNolan.com.

Made in the USA
Lexington, KY
18 August 2018